GW01237986

A YEAR OF
THERMAL COOKING

by

'Mr D' (Dave Knowles)

the Thermal Cook

More recipes for the eco-friendly Mr D's Thermal Cooker

A Year of Thermal Cooking
ISBN: 978-0-9565359-9-3

Published by Little Knoll Press
www.LittleKnollPress.co.uk
Email: mail@LittleKnollPress.co.uk

First published in 2013   © Little Knoll Press 2013

Printed and bound in Great Britain by
Hobbs the Printers Ltd
Southampton

Welcome to the world of Thermal Cooking

 It's not a new science – there are records of thermal cooking in Medieval times, and anyone who has watched BBC's 'Wartime Farm' will know about cooking in a hay box - but it is a way of cooking that Mr D's Thermal Cooker, by using vacuum technology, takes into another dimension.

Jen and I started selling Mr D's cookers in 2010, and now there are thousands of cooks out there, preparing meals in their Mr D's - at home, in caravans, boats, motorhomes, beach huts, tents and lorry cabs.

After initial heating on the hob, the food slow cooks in Mr D's without any power, and then keeps safely hot for hours.
This means a meal can easily be taken out, while still cooking, to friends, to the beach, on walks, shoots, fishing, to rugby fixtures, and even to the office.

Lots of Mr D's are simply used at home – we use ours all the time – but we never cease to be surprised at the places where our cookers go. They cross the Atlantic, race around the Fastnet, bump across the Sahara in the back of Land Rovers, have worked as 'the kitchen' on the spray-swept floor of a cross-Atlantic rowing boat, and graced the table at the opera.

The vacuum insulation also makes Mr D's ideal where a steady temperature needs to be kept, for instance to make yoghurt, cheese or beer, to keep food chilled or make ice-cream.

Whether you are already a committed thermal cook or whether you are new to it, we hope this book will give you lots of inspiration to get cooking with a Mr D's, and save time and money, whilst getting the best out of your ingredients.

Please keep sharing your stories and recipes, and ask to join the gallery of Mr D's owners on
www.MrDsCookware.com
Facebook: **MrDsFanPage.co.uk**
and **YouTube.com/MrDsKitchen**

Mr D

Mr D's Thermal Cooker uses a two pot system:

The Outer Pot - a stainless steel vacuum insulated pot that will maintain the heat in the food inside the inner pot, allowing it to slow cook for hours and then keep at a safe cooking temperature for hours longer. The insulation will also keep cold food cold, and when ice and salt are used, will lower the temperature further - ideal for making ice-cream.

The Inner Pot - a stainless steel pot with a heavy bottom, suitable for use on the hob - gas, electric, induction, or radiant (such as a pot bellied stove or Aga).

Accessories

Top Pot - sits inside the top half of the Inner Pot to let you cook two dishes at the same time. The Top Pot also has a heavy bottom, suitable for use on the hob - gas, electric, or induction.

Bread & Cake Tins - in stainless steel with easy-to-close lids and hinged handles for lifting out of the Inner Pot while still hot.

Trivet - for use with the bread and cake tins, the trivet has a flat top to keep your cooking tin level within the Inner Pot.

Carry handle - allows you to carry your Mr D's in one hand. NOTE: fit the carry handle with the logo mid centre and pull the straps tight on each side, after clipping the handle into place.

Care Instructions

Inner Pot - wash and rinse the Inner Pot and lid thoroughly before first use and after each use. You can put Mr D's in the dishwasher at normal wash temperatures.

Food is less likely to get stuck on the surface of the Inner Pot because of the method of cooking, but if you get a stubborn mark you can use a soft plastic type of scourer.

Outer Pot - the Outer Pot should be wiped clean with a soft cloth, dampened with warm water and mild detergent. Do not put the Outer Pot in water or on a hot surface.

To clean the Outer Pot lid, remove it by lifting it slightly and pulling forward to release the hinge. Wipe clean.

Do not use abrasive cleansers or scrubbers since they may dull the finish. Do not use bleach or cleaners containing chlorine on any parts of the product.

For more information or to buy these items, see contact details on the last page.

How it works

Simply place your prepared ingredients in the Inner Pot and heat on a stove. After it comes to the boil, reduce heat, cover, and simmer for 10 - 15 minutes. Turn off heat and transfer the Inner Pot, with the lid on, into the insulated Outer Pot and shut the lid. That's it - the heat is retained and your meal will continue slowly cooking for hours until you are ready to eat.

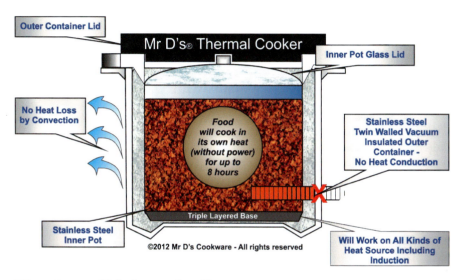

How hot will it keep food?

Due to vacuum insulation, there is only a heat loss of 3-4°C per hour. This means the Inner Pot of food that you have put into the Outer Pot at boiling temperature will gently and slowly cook for hours without constant attention. For example a 75 - 80% full Inner Pot will still have a temperature around 70°C after 6 hours.

You can also keep foods **chilled** for an extended period by placing ice cubes (in a sealed plastic bag) in the bottom of the inner pot and placing the food on top.

NOTE: Do not freeze the Inner Pot as the base is constructed of layers of dissimilar metals for maximum heat and cold retention and they will expand and contract at differing rates. However, you can chill the Inner Pot in a refrigerator.

Awards

Voted 'No. 1 Live Aboard Accessory' by Sailing Today. Practical Boat Owner picked Mr D's as their 2012 Green Award Winner.

Recipes

Over the past year I have cooked and recorded one new recipe a week. Those of you who subscribe to Mr D's email newsletter will have received these recipes weekly, but many have asked for them compiled into a book. Here they are in the order in which they were posted - i.e. the recipe for week 1 is on page 1 etc.

A further alphabetical index can be found at the back of the book.

Mr D's Jubilee Cake

Recipe 01 - 11th June 2012

The first recipe is for Mr D's Jubilee Cake, which was won by Jacquie Gardner who entered a competition held by us at The Crick Boat Show. The cake itself is a whiskey fruit cake and the recipe could be used for a Christmas Cake or just a tea time treat any time of the year.

375 g mixed dried fruit

185 ml brown sugar

1 tsp mixed spice

grated rind of an orange

125 ml water or orange juice

60 ml whiskey

125 g butter

2 large eggs, lightly beaten

150 g self raising flour

150 g plain flour

½ tsp bicarbonate of soda

For this recipe you will need a Mr D's cake tin and trivet available from MrDsCookware.com

1. Cut two circles of baking paper to fit the cake tin*, one for the base and one for the top. Grease the tin and line the base with one circle. Leave to one side until needed.

2. Place the dried fruit into a saucepan with the brown sugar, mixed spice, orange rind, water, whiskey and butter.

3. Bring the mixture to the boil and simmer uncovered for 5 minutes.

4. Allow the mixture to cool. This is very important as the eggs will cook if the mixture is hot.

5. Once cooled mix the eggs into the mixture.

6. Stir in the sifted flour and bicarbonate of soda.

7. Spoon the mixture into the prepared cake tin and put the second greased circle (that you cut earlier) on the top of the mixture before putting the lid on the cake tin*.

8. Place the cake tin on a the trivet* inside the inner pot.

9. Add enough boiling water to come ¾ the way up the side of the cake tin and bring back to the boil.

10. Put the lid on the inner pot and turn down the heat. Simmer gently for 35 to 40 minutes.

11. Turn off the heat and transfer the inner pot into the vacuum-insulated outer container.

12. Close the lid and leave to cook for a minimum of 4 to 5 hours. Ideally the cake should be left to cook overnight.

Venison Shanks with Red Wine
Recipe 02 - 18th June 2012

This recipe uses venison shanks bought from our local farm shop. I cooked the shanks in red wine and served them with lovely smooth mashed potatoes.

- 4 venison shanks
- 750 ml red wine
- 2 garlic cloves, crushed
- 8 juniper berries
- 4 cloves
- 1 cinnamon stick
- ½ lemon, cut into four pieces

- 2 sprigs of fresh thyme
- 200 g smoked bacon lardons, fried until starting to become crispy.
- 2 onions, roughly chopped
- 2 beef stock cubes
- 3 tbsp redcurrant jelly
- 1 tsp freshly ground black pepper

1. Put all the ingredients in a container and leave to marinade over night in the fridge.
2. Place the venison shanks and the marinade into the inner pot.
3. Bring to the boil, skimming any impurities from the surface.
4. Turn down the heat and simmer for 10 minutes with the lid on.
5. Place the inner pot into the insulated outer container and shut the lid.
6. Leave it to thermal cook without power for a minimum of 5 hours, longer would be good.
7. When ready, check the seasoning and adjust if necessary then serve with fresh greens and smooth mashed potatoes.

Serves 4   *minimum thermal cooking time without power: 5 hours*

Lamb with Creamed Asparagus
Recipe 03 - 25th June 2012

Lamb and asparagus are my favourites.

The original recipe appeared in Waitrose Weekend (their weekly newspaper) but I have changed some of the ingredients and the method to work in your thermal cooker.

- 1 tbsp olive oil
- 750 g lamb leg, cubed
- 1 medium onion, chopped
- 1.5 litres water
- 450 g asparagus, trimmed

- 2 packets cream of asparagus soup mix
- 2 tbsp fresh mint chopped
- 250 g small Chantenay carrots, trimmed
- juice of one lemon

1. Put the oil in the inner pot and heat.
2. Add the lamb in batches and brown.
3. Remove the lamb and put it to one side for later.
4. Add the onions and cook until soft.
5. Remove them and keep for later.
6. Put the water in the inner pot and bring to the boil
7. Add the asparagus, bring back to the boil then simmer for 5 minutes.
8. Remove the asparagus and put to one side for later.
9. Add the soup mix and stir well to make sure it is dissolved.
10. Add all the other ingredients including the lamb and onions but not the asparagus. Stir well.
11. Bring to the boil.
12. Turn down the heat and simmer for 5 minutes with the lid on.
13. Place the inner pot into the insulated outer container and shut the lid.
14. Leave it the thermal cook without power for a minimum of 3 hours.
15. When ready, check the seasoning and adjust if necessary then add the asparagus and bring back to the boil.
16. Serve with new potatoes.

Serves 4   minimum thermal cooking time without power: 3 hours

3

Pork Mole
Recipe 04 - 7th July 2012

Mole is the generic name for a number of sauces used in Mexican cuisine, as well as for dishes based on these sauces. Three states in Mexico claim to be the origin of mole, Puebla, Oaxaca and Tlaxcala.

Moles come in various flavors and ingredients, with chilli peppers as the common factor. However, the classic mole version is the variety called mole poblano, which is a dark red or brown sauce served over meat. I have used pork in this dish but you could use chicken if you wished.

2 tbsp rapeseed oil	1 tsp ground cinnamon
1.5 kg shoulder of pork	2 tbsp malt vinegar
3 medium onions, finely chopped	400 g tin plum tomatoes
3 cloves garlic, finely chopped	2 tsp Chipotle Paste
1 dried chilli	1.5 litres chicken stock
2 tsp ground cumin	3 tbsp smooth peanut butter
2 tsp ground coriander	75 g dark chocolate, grated

1. Put the oil in the inner pot and heat.
2. Add the pork and brown on all sides.
3. Remove the pork and put it to one side for later.
4. Add the onions and cook until soft.
5. Add the garlic and spices and cook for 5 minutes.
6. Add the vinegar and tomatoes and cook for 3 minutes
7. Add all the other ingredients and bring to the boil stirring frequently.
8. Once boiling carefully lower the pork into the sauce making sure that it is covered. If not, top up with a little water.
9. Bring back to the boil.
10. Turn down the heat and simmer for 5 minutes with the lid on.
11. Place the inner pot into the insulated outer container and shut the lid.
12. Leave it the thermal cook without power for a minimum of 4 hours longer if possible.
13. When ready, check the seasoning and adjust if necessary then either slice or shred the pork.
14. Serve on rice with some of the sauce poured over the meat.

Serves 4 - 6   minimum thermal cooking time without power: 4 hours

Rogan Josh Lamb Shanks

Recipe 05 - 9th July 2012

There are other versions of Rogan Josh Lamb Shanks but this is my version. To get the best from this recipe you need to slash the lamb shanks a few times to allow the spices to penetrate and, like all lamb shanks recipes, this one needs a long cooking time to tenderise the meat.

- 2 inch piece of ginger
- 6 cloves garlic, chopped
- 4 tbsp water vegetable oil
- 12 cardamom pods
- 2 bay leaves
- 6 cloves
- ½ tsp peppercorns
- 2 onions, chopped
- 1 tsp ground coriander

- 2 tsp ground cumin
- 4 tsp paprika
- 1 tsp cayenne pepper
- 1 ½ tsp salt
- 250 g plain yogurt
- 400 g tin chopped tomatoes
- 2 to 4 lamb shanks, depending on how many you are cooking for

1. Blend together the ginger, garlic and the 4 tablespoons of water.
2. Put the inner pot on a medium heat and add 4 tablespoons of vegetable oil.
3. Add the lamb shanks and brown all over 2 at a time. Then put them to one side while you prepare the sauce to cook them in.
4. Put the cardamom, bay leaves, cloves, peppercorns and cinnamon in the inner pot and stir for 30 seconds.
5. Add the chopped onions and cook for 5 minutes.
6. Add the ginger and garlic mixture and stir for 30 seconds.
7. Stir in 1 tablespoon of the yogurt and mix well.
8. Slowly add the rest of the yogurt and the tin of tomatoes stirring as it is added. Cook for 3 minutes.
9. Place the shanks into the sauce making sure that they are cover. If the sauce does not cover them, add a little water.
10. Bring to the boil before turning down to a simmer.
11. Put on the lid and simmer for 10 minutes before placing the inner pot into the insulated outer container.
12. Shut the lid and thermal cook without power until the shanks are tender. This will be 5 to 6 hours.
13. Serve with rice and naan bread.

Serves 2 - 4   minimum thermal cooking time without power: 5 hours

Sausage & Lentils

Recipe 06 - 16th July 2012

This is real comfort food and so easy to make in your thermal cooker. There are so many different types for sausages so choose which you like for this recipe. I am using wild garlic and black pepper sausages bought from our local farm shop. These I am going to cook with green lentils, chopped rosemary and red wine.
I am using tinned lentils, but you can use dried if you wish.

- 3 tbsp olive oil
- 10 to 12 of sausages of your choice
- 1 onion, chopped
- 2 cloves garlic, thinly sliced
- 1 tbsp rosemary, chopped
- 2 x 400 g tins tomatoes. chopped
- 16 juniper berries
- ½ tsp grated nutmeg

- 2 bay leaves
- 1 dried chilli, crushed
- 185 ml red wine
- 20 ml water
- 2 x 410 g tins of green lentils
- Salt and pepper
- 3 tbsp olive oil

1. Heat the oil in the inner pot, add the sausages in batches and cook over a medium heat until they are browned on all sides.
2. Remove the sausages and keep warm.
3. Add the onion and garlic and cook until the onion is softened.
4. Stir in the rosemary and tomatoes and cook for 5 minutes until the juice is thickened.
5. Add the juniper berries, nutmeg, bay leaves, chilli, wine and water.
6. Bring to the boil and then add the sausages and lentils.
7. Stir and bring back to the boil., put the lid on and turn down the heat and simmer for 2 to 3 minutes.
8. Put the inner pot into the insulated outer container and shut the lid.
9. Thermal cook without power for a minimum of 2 hours.
10. Serve with crusty bread.

Serves 2 - 4   minimum thermal cooking time without power: 2 hours

Chicken Adobo
Recipe 07 - 22nd July 2012

The first time I tried chicken adobo was when some Filipino friends in Abu Dhabi made it for me. I then went on to learn that there is no defined recipe as every mum in the Philippines seems to have her own version. The basics of garlic, soy and vinegar stay the same, but the balance of these ingredients are altered to suit each person who makes it. There are even one or two who add coconut milk to the dish but as far as I can see this is not acceptable to many.

1 kg chicken pieces thighs and legs	4-6 cloves garlic, peeled and crushed
250 ml rice vinegar	3 bay leaves
125 ml light soy sauce	3 birdseye chillies, 2left whole, 1 chopped
75 ml dark soy sauce	
75 ml of Sprite	1 tsp freshly ground black pepper

1. Put some cold water (to cool it down) in the insulated outer container and shut the lid and leave to stand in a cool place for about 15 minutes.
2. Wash the chicken pieces well, put them in the inner pot, add the rest of the ingredients, mix well and put on the lid.
3. After removing the water from the outer container, put the inner pot in and shut the lid. Keep in a cool place for a minimum of 2 hours.
4. When ready to cook the adobo, remove the inner pot and leave the lid of the outer container open so that it can warm up as you are going to use it next for cooking.
5. Bring to the inner pot to the boil.
6. Once boiling, skim off any impurities that have formed on the surface and then turn the heat down to a simmer.
7. Simmer for 5 minutes with the lid on before placing the inner pot into the outer insulated container. If the outer container still feels cold, warm it with a little warm water (not boiling) before putting the inner pot in.
8. Shut the lid and leave to thermal cook without power for a minimum of 3 hours.
9. Serve with rice, which you can cook at the same time as the adobo in a top pot if you have one.

NOTE: you can marinate the adobo in the fridge prior to cooking if you prefer.

Serves 4 - 6   minimum thermal cooking time without power: 3 hours

Chinese Five-Spice Beef

Recipe 08 - 30th July 2012

This is such an easy-to-make dish and has all the flavours of Asia. If you like Chinese food, you will love this one.

450 g lean rump steak, cubed (if you want to double this to feed 8 do not change the amounts of the other ingredients)

350 ml orange juice

350 ml beef stock

225 g Chinese leaves, coarsely sliced

1 large onion, cut into thin slices

2 tbsp teriyaki sauce

2 tsp Chinese five-spice powder

2 tsp chili sauce with garlic

To serve

1 tbsp vegetable oil (double this if making for 8 people)

600 g fresh egg noodles (for 4 people double for 8)*

300 g stir fry mixed vegetables (for 4 people double for 8)

* If using dried egg noodles add them to boiling water for 2 minutes before draining and then stir frying.

1. Put all the ingredients except the noodles and stir fry vegetables in the inner pot.
2. Bring to the inner pot to the boil.
3. Once boiling, skim off any impurities that have formed on the surface and then turn the heat down to a simmer.
4. Simmer for 5 minutes with the lid on before placing the inner pot into the outer insulated container.
5. Shut the lid and leave to thermal cook without power for 2 to 4 hours.
6. Just before serving add 1 tbsp (2 tbsp if making for 8 people) of vegetable oil in a heavy based frying pan or wok.
7. Heat the oil on a high heat until it shimmers.
8. Carefully add the noodles and stir fry vegetables and stir fry for 3 minutes.
9. Portion the noodles onto plates and add the five-spice beef on top.

serves: 4   *minimum thermal cooking time without power: 6 hours*

Hong Bak (Black Pork)

Recipe 09 - 5th August 2012

This is a recipe I used in a demonstration at The New Forest Show. It is a version of red-cooked pork and well worth a try if you like Chinese food.

6 tbsp cooking oil	4 hard boiled eggs (optional)
300 g shallots, thinly sliced	3 tbsp dark soy sauce
3 cloves garlic	3 tbsp light soy sauce
1 tbsp sugar	225 ml water
500 g shoulder pork with skin cut into 4cm cubes	

1. Heat the oil in the inner pot and add the shallots. Cook until golden and crispy.
2. Remove the onions with a slotted spoon and put on paper towels for later.
3. Remove all but 1 tablespoon of oil from the inner pot.
4. Add the garlic and cook until it is fragrant, being careful not to let it burn or it will go bitter.
5. Add the sugar and stir continuously until it melts and caramelises (goes slightly darker).
6. Add the dark soy sauce and the pork. Stir making sure that the pork is well covered.
7. Add the light soy sauce (this is for seasoning), fried shallots and the water. Make sure that the pork is covered and if not add a little more water.
8. Bring the inner pot up to the boil, stirring occasionally. At this stage add the eggs if using them.
9. Place the lid on. Turn down the heat and simmer for 5 minutes stirring occasionally.
10. Place the inner pot into the vacuum-insulated outer Thermal container, shut the lid and leave while you start the rice in the top pot.
11. If not using a top pot leave to cook for a minimum of 2 hours.

Cooking the rice in the top pot.

1. Add the rice and water to the top pot and bring to the boil, stir and turn down the heat and simmer for 1 minute.
2. Turn off the heat, open the vacuum-insulated outer Thermal container and place the top pot into the inner pot.
3. Put the lid on the top pot and shut the lid of the outer container.
4. Leave to thermal cook without power for a minimum of 2 hours.

Serves: 4 - 8   minimum thermal cooking time without power: 2 hours

Steak and Kidney Pudding
Recipe 10 - 13th August 2012

We have been making steak and kidney pudding in a pudding bowl for a number of years but this one is cooked in the top pot. For this recipe I have used two tins of ready made steak and kidney but you could use uncooked steak and kidney with some nice onion gravy.

Vegetarian version:
Use vegetarian suet and fill with a medley of vegetables, exotic mushrooms and a vegetable stock..

NOTE: If you do not have a top pot you can make this recipe in a pudding bowl on a trivet. Don't forget to cover the bowl so drips of water do not get on the top of the pudding.

For suet dough:

250 g self-raising flour

125 g shredded suet

½ tsp salt

180 ml cold water

For steak and kidney filling:

2 x 400 g ready made steak and kidney

If using uncooked ingredients

500 g steak, cubed

250 g pig's kidney (or calf's kidney if preferred)

2 tbsp flour seasoned with salt and pepper to taste

3 tbsp cold water

1 tbsp Worcester sauce

Vegetables

300 g small new potatoes, cut in half if too large

200 g carrots cut into 2 cm pieces

14

Suet dough

1. Put 2 cups of flour, 1 cup of suet and ½ teaspoon salt in a mixing bowl and mix together.
2. Make a hollow in the middle of the mixture, pour ¼ of the water into the hollow and spoon the dry ingredients into the water until it is absorbed.
3. Repeat with two further ¼ amounts of water. The mixture should now be bound into a ball of soft dough. If there is still some loose flour and suet, add a little more water to unite with the dough.
4. Grease the top pot and cut a piece of greaseproof paper in the base. Don't forget to grease the lid.
5. Use 2/3 of the dough to line the top pot sides and base, making sure there are no holes in the dough wall. Keep the remaining 1/3 of the suet dough for the pudding lid.
6. Fill with the two tins of steak and kidney. If using uncooked steak & kidney go to 'Using uncooked steak & kidney' below.
7. Shape the remaining 1/3 of suet dough to make a lid for the pudding, position it on top of the meat filling and press the dough edges together to form a seal.
8. Place a circle of greaseproof or baking paper on top of the pudding.
9. Put potatoes and carrots in the bottom of the inner pot and fill it with boiling water up to 6.5 cms from the top edge.
10. Place the top pot into the inner pot and bring back to the boil.
11. Turn down the heat and simmer for 25 - 30 minutes.
12. Put the inner pot into the vacuum-insulated outer Thermal pot, close the outer pot lid and leave to thermal cook without power for a minimum of 4 hours. If Mr D's Thermal Cooker is left unopened you can serve this dish up to 6½ hours after starting the thermal cooking.
13. Serve with the potatoes and carrots.

Using uncooked steak & kidney.

1. Toss the cubed steak and kidney in the seasoned flour.
2. Heat 2 tablespoons of cooking oil in a cooking pan, add the meat and turn it to seal.
3. Add half the quantity of meat at a time so that the pan keeps hot enough to seal the meat quickly. When sealed it will be light brown. Take the pan off the hob.
4. Add 3 tablespoons of cold water and 1 tablespoon of Worcester sauce. Stir so that the flour absorbs the water and Worcester sauce and mixes into a gravy.
5. Fill with the lined top pot with the steak and kidney.
6. Go to 7 above.

serves: 4   *minimum thermal cooking time without power: 4 hours*

Chicken Cacciatore
Recipe 11 - 20th August 2012

Cacciatore means 'hunter', so this is probably is what the hunter's wife would cook for her husband when he returned from a day's hunting.
This is my version of this famous Italian classic tasty tomato and chicken dish. Cacciatore can be served with a rustic bread or pasta.

1 kg chicken portions, legs and thighs

2 onions, chopped

2 cloves garlic, crushed

125 ml white wine

1 tbsp white wine vinegar

125 ml chicken stock

2 x 400 g tins chopped tomatoes

2 tbsp tomato puree

2 tsp dried oregano

1 tsp brown sugar

100 g stoned black olives

4 anchovy fillets

salt & pepper to season

To Serve

225 g pasta or crusty bread

1. Add all the ingredients except for the salt, pepper and pasta to the inner pot.
2. Mix everything and bring to the boil.
3. Turn the heat down and simmer for 5 minutes with the lid on.
4. Turn off the heat and put the inner pot into the insulated outer container.
5. Shut the lid and thermal cook without power for a minimum of 2 hours.
6. Before serving check the seasoning, adding salt and pepper if necessary.
7. Serve with pasta and crusty bread.

serves: 4   minimum thermal cooking time without power: 2 hours

Gammon with Cumberland Sauce

Recipe 12 - 27th August 2012

I am often asked about cooking a piece of gammon in the thermal cooker so I though this week I would let you know how we do it. There is also a Cumberland sauce to go with it but this will need to be cooked separately and not in your thermal cooker.

1.5 kg smoked or unsmoked gammon joint

1 large carrot, cut into chunks

1 bay leaf

1 medium onion sliced

Cumberland Sauce

1 orange

1 lemon

15 g fresh ginger root, grated

225 g redcurrant jelly

125 ml port

2 tsp whole Dijon mustard

Salt & freshly ground black pepper

1. Add the gammon, carrot, onion and bay leaf to the inner pot, fill with water up to about 2 to 3 cms from the top.
2. Bring to the boil, skim off any scum from the surface, then turn the heat down and simmer for 10 minutes with the lid on.
3. Turn off the heat and put the inner pot into the insulated outer container., shut the lid and thermal cook without power for a minimum of 3 hours.

The Cumberland Sauce

1. Use a zester to remove rind from the orange and lemon, then use a small sharp knife to remove the white pith and cut the rind into long thin strands.
2. Juice the orange and lemon and keep to one side for later.
3. Place rind in a medium saucepan, cover with water and bring to the boil over high heat.
4. Reduce heat to medium and simmer, stirring occasionally, for 5 minutes or until rind softens.
5. Drain and return rind to the saucepan, add the orange and lemon juice, ginger, red currant jelly, port and mustard., then cook, stirring over medium heat for 4 minutes or until mixture melts.
6. Reduce heat to low and simmer, stirring occasionally, for 6-8 minutes or until sauce thickens slightly.
7. Taste and season with salt and pepper before transferring to a serving jug.
8. Leave to cool or serve warm with the gammon.

Blueberry and Pineapple Crumble

Recipe 13 - 3rd September 2012

For a change this week I am cooking a blueberry and crushed pineapple crumble.
You will need either a top pot or a cake tin for this recipe. If you are using a top pot, the crumble can cook while your main meal is cooking

200 g blueberries, fresh or frozen

432 g tin crushed pineapple, in natural juice

For the Crumble
125 g plain flour, sifted

30 g caster sugar

30 g dark muscovado sugar

75 g butter, chilled, cut into cubes. It is important that the butter is cold, or it won't crumble properly.

75 g rolled porridge oats

under it.

1. Add the blueberries and crushed pineapple (with the juice) to the top pot and bring to the boil.
2. Turn the heat down and simmer for 5 minutes while you make the crumble mix.
3. For the crumble mix, add everything except the oats to a bowl and rub together until a crumble is formed.
4. Add in the oats and mix well.
5. Sprinkle the crumble over the top of the fruit.
6. Place the top pot into the inner pot containing your main meal, which should already be in the insulated outer container starting to cook. If you are just cooking the crumble fill the inner pot with boiling water so the water just touches the base of the top pot.
7. Shut the lid of the outer container and leave to cook without power for a minimum of 2 hours. If the main meal needs longer than 2 hours base the cooking time on this.
8. When ready serve with crème fraîche.

serves: 6   *minimum thermal cooking time without power: 2 hours*

Pot Roast Pork

Recipe 14 - 10th September 2012

I bought a nice piece of pork the other day, about 1 kg in size and wanted to do something rather than roasting it in the conventional way. I therefore decided to pot roast it in white wine with leeks which are now in season.

1 kg boned and rolled leg or shoulder joint of pork

1 tsp dried or fresh thyme

1 tsp dried sage

1 tsp dried rosemary

2 tsp fennel seeds

2 cloves garlic, sliced

2 tbsp rapeseed oil

2 onions, peeled and cut into wedges

5 juniper berries , crushed

1 tsp golden caster sugar

1 tbsp white wine vinegar

4 whole leeks, trimmed then each cut into 4 cm lengths

750 ml white wine

1. Mix together the thyme, sage, rosemary and fennel seeds.
2. Untie and unroll the pork joint then lay the sliced garlic on the meat.
3. Sprinkle all of the herbs over the meat evenly and rub them in.
4. Retie the meat.
5. Heat the rapeseed oil in the inner pot and carefully place the rolled pork in. Brown the pork on all sides.
6. Add the onions, then continue to cook for about 5 minutes until they start to soften.
7. Add the crushed juniper berries, sprinkle with the sugar and add the vinegar.
8. Add the leeks so they are around the meat.
9. Pour over the wine. If it does not cover the meat top up with water.
10. Bring to the boil and then turn down the heat and simmer for 10 minutes.
11. Turn off the heat and put the inner pot into the insulated outer container.
12. Shut the lid and thermal cook without power for a minimum of 4 hours.
13. Before serving, check the seasoning, adding salt and pepper if necessary.
14. Serve with either boiled or mashed potatoes.

NOTE: This meat is delicious cold with salad.

serves: 4   minimum thermal cooking time without power: 4 - 6 hours

Thai Chicken Risotto

Recipe 15 - 16th September 2012

This is a great risotto for those who like Thai flavours. You could substitute or add prawns, and the addition of peas would be nice.

2 tbsp vegetable oil

1 tbsp butter

1 large onion, diced

1 clove garlic, finely chopped

2 chicken breasts, cut into cubes

1 tbsp Thai green paste

3 tbsp fish sauce

250 gm risotto rice

800 ml chicken stock

½ tsp fresh ground pepper

1. Put the oil and butter in the inner pot.
2. Heat over a medium heat until the butter melts.
3. Add the onions and garlic and cook until the onion is soft. Don't let it colour.
4. Add the chicken and Thai paste.
5. Cook stirring for 1 minute until the chicken is sealed.
6. Add the rice and stir well.
7. Add the stock, fish sauce and pepper. Stir and bring to the boil.
8. Once boiling turn down to a simmer for 2 to 3 minutes.
9. Give the mixture a stir then put on the lid
10. Turn off the heat and put the inner pot into the insulated outer container
11. Shut the lid and thermal cook without power for a minimum of 1 hour.
12. Before serving check the seasoning and adjust if necessary.

serves: 4   minimum thermal cooking time without power: 1 hour

Boeuf Bourguignon
Recipe 16 - 24th September 2012

With Autumn here, this recipe sent to me by Natalie, one my first customers to buy a thermal cooker, is the is ideal meal to impress your friends.

The brandy was not in the original but I found it gives a added depth of flavour. You can of course leave it out if you wish.

2 tbsp olive oil	250 g small button mushrooms
50 g butter	60 ml brandy (this is optional but does give the dish great depth of flavour)
1 kg beef, cut into cubes	
3 cloves garlic, crushed	1 x 750 ml bottle of strong red wine
1 large onion, sliced	beef stock if needed
12 bacon rashers, chopped	2 bay leaves
1 large carrot, chopped into smallish pieces	½ tsp fresh ground pepper
	1 small bunch thyme
2 tbsp plain flour	salt to season
2 tbsp tomato puree	

1. Heat the olive oil in the inner pot over a medium heat.
2. Add the butter and in two batches brown the meat in the inner pot.
3. Once browned remove the meat and put to one side.
4. Add the garlic, onion, bacon, carrot and cook over a medium heat until the onion is soft.
5. Mix in the flour and cook for one minute, stirring all the time.
6. Add the tomato puree and mix well using a little of the wine to loosen it if needed. Cook for 1 minute.
7. Put the meat back in, add the brandy, mushrooms and the bottle of red wine. Stir the mixture and if everything is not covered, top up with beef stock.
8. Add the bay leaves, pepper and small bunch of thyme. Put on the lid and bring to the boil. Once boiling skim off any impurities that have formed on the surface.
9. Turn down the heat and simmer for 5 minutes.
10. Turn off the heat and put the inner pot into the outer insulated container. Shut the lid and thermal cook without power for a minimum of 3 hours. Longer would be better.
11. Serve with potatoes and vegetables of your choice.

serves: 4   *minimum thermal cooking time without power: 3 hours*

Savoury Fish Crumble

Recipe 17 - 1st October 2012

The savoury crumble mixture in this recipe can be used on anything that would normally have a potato topping. The important thing with the crumble is not to over work it or it will become a gooey mass rather than like breadcrumbs.

You should find that 2.4L of water will just creep up the side of the top pot by about 1 cm when in place. You may need to adjust the amount slightly especially if you are not using a Mr D's Thermal Cooker.

Savoury crumble:

75 g flour

75 g rolled grains (oats, wheat, barley rice flakes)

1 tsp mixed herbs

60 g grated Parmesan

45 ml oil (olive, rapeseed or hemp oil)

White sauce and fish:

425 ml cold milk

20 g plain flour

40 g butter

400 g mixed fish or seafood (mussels, prawns, squid etc.)

salt & pepper

1. Combine the crumble ingredients into a bowl. Mix well by rubbing until the mixture resembles breadcrumbs and place to one side for later.
2. Add 2.4L of water (ideally boiling) to the inner pot and bring to the boil with the lid on.
3. Once boiling, place the inner pot into the outer insulated container and shut the lid.
4. Add the cold milk, plain flour, butter, herbs and Parmesan to the top pot.
5. Gradually bring to the boil stirring continuously until it thickens.
6. Turn down the heat and simmer for 5 minutes stirring occasionally.
7. Check the seasoning and adjust with salt and pepper if necessary.
8. Add the fish to the white sauce and heat for a few minutes, stirring occasionally until you see the odd bubble coming from the white sauce.
9. Sprinkle over the savory crumble mixture and place the lid on the top pot.
10. Remove the inner pot and bring back to the boil.
11. Once boiling, place the top pot into the inner pot and turn the heat down to a simmer.
12. Simmer for 3 minutes and then place the inner pot and top pot into the outer insulated container.
13. Shut the lid and thermal cook without power for a minimum of 2 hours.

serves: 2 - 3   minimum thermal cooking time without power: 2 hours

Saffron Chicken Curry

Recipe 18 - 8th October 2012

This dish is based on a recipe from one of my favourite cookbooks "curry, curry curry" by Ranjit Rai. I have made a few alterations and added the potatoes. In his book Ranjit Rai says that he is not sure if the dish came from Spain or went to Spain but no matter, if you like saffron this is certainly one to try.

1.6 kg chicken, jointed	20 g blanched almonds
75 ml cooking oil	1 tsp chilli powder
20 g saffron	250 g small potatoes, halved
35 ml warm milk	*For rice* 2 cups of basmati rice
300 ml coconut milk	3 cups of water
165 g yogurt	
2 onions. roughly chopped	
1 ½ tsp turmeric	
3 cm fresh ginger root, peeled and roughly chopped	
1 tsp salt	

1. Add the saffron to the warm milk and set aside.
2. Put the coconut milk, yogurt, chopped onions, turmeric, ginger, salt, almonds and chilli powder in a blender and liquidize.
3. Heat the oil in the inner pot and add the chicken pieces in batches. Fry until they are light brown.
4. Add the contents of the liquidizer to the chicken in the inner pot and bring to the boil, stirring occasionally.
5. Turn down the heat, pour over the saffron and milk. Simmer for 5 minutes with the lid on.
6. Place the inner pot into the outer Thermal container, shut the lid. Leave while you start the rice in the top pot. If not using a top pot leave to cook for a minimum of 2 hours.

Cooking rice in the top pot.

1. Add the rice and water to the top pot and bring to the boil. Stir then turn down the heat and simmer for 1 minute.
2. Turn off the heat, open the vacuum-insulated outer Thermal container and place the top pot into the inner pot, put the lid on the top pot, shut the lid of the outer container and leave to thermal cook without power for a minimum of 2 hours.

Add naan bread and a vegetable curry to serve a feast for 4

Minimum thermal cooking time without power: 2 hours

Game Stew

At this time of the year you can't beat a hearty stew. This simple mixed game stew is just the thing to eat with your friends on a cold autumn evening.

I like to serve with some crusty bread to mop up the rick gravy this stew makes after the long slow thermal cooking.

50 g butter

100 g chorizo, cut into 1 cm cubes

500 g mixed game

3 carrots, chopped into chunks

500 g small potatoes, halved

8 shallots, peeled

1 x 750 ml bottle red wine

2 tbsp redcurrant jelly

2 tbsp beef gravy granules (this is used instead of stock and will help thicken the sauce)

to serve:

vegetables of your choice

1. In the inner pot, add the butter and the chorizo. Cook on a medium heat for five minutes, stirring occasionally.
2. Turn up the heat and add the game in batches until sealed all over. Remove each batch when sealed with a slotted spoon and set aside.
3. Once all the meat has been sealed, add it all back into the inner pot.
4. Add all the other ingredients and bring to the boil stirring occasionally.
5. Skim any impurities from the surface and turn down to a simmer.
6. Simmer for 5 minutes with the lid on.
7. Place the inner pot into the vacuum-insulated outer Thermal container, shut the lid. Leave to cook for a minimum of 3 hours.
8. Before serving check the seasoning and add salt and pepper if necessary.
9. Serve with vegetables of your choice.

serves: 4 - 6   minimum thermal cooking time without power: 3 hours

Pork in Cider
Recipe 20 - 22nd October 2012

Pork and cider together make a delicious thermally cooked meal that can be eaten all year round.
This meal is very easy to make and can be left cooking in your thermal cooker until you are ready to eat.
Serve with seasonal vegetables and a sprinkling of chopped parsley for a meal to eat any day of the week.

2 tbsp rapeseed oil

1 kg pork shoulder , diced

2 onions, sliced

2 celery sticks, roughly chopped

3 parsnips , cut into chunks

2 bay leaves

3 tbsp chicken gravy granules

500 g small new potatoes

330 ml bottle cider

850 ml water

1 handful parsley, chopped

1. Heat the oil in the inner pot and brown the meat in batches, then set aside.
2. Add the onions, celery and parsnips with the bay leaves and fry until golden brown.
3. Sprinkle in the gravy granules and give a good stir.
4. Add the pork and any juices back to the dish.
5. Add the potatoes.
6. Pour in the cider and water, making sure everything is covered. If not add a little more water.
7. Bring to the boil, stirring occasionally. Skim any impurities from the surface.
8. Turn down the heat and simmer for 5 minutes with the lid on.
9. Place the inner pot into the vacuum-insulated outer Thermal container, shut the lid. Leave to cook for a minimum of 2 hours.
10. Before serving, check the seasoning and adjust if necessary.
11. Garnish with the parsley and serve with vegetables of your choice.

serves: 4   minimum thermal cooking time without power: 2 hours

5th of November Chilli

Recipe 21 - 29th October 2012

This chilli is slightly different as it is made with beer rather than water. This with the cumin and oregano gives it a great depth of flavour.
The recipe will give 8 good portions but if you need to feed more then just multiply up the ingredients.

2 tbsp olive oil

500 g minced beef

2 large onions, chopped

1 green pepper, chopped

2 cloves garlic, crushed

2 tsp ground cumin

2 tsp dried oregano

2 x 400 g tins chopped tomatoes

2 x 400 g tins kidney beans

175 g tomato puree

175 ml of beer (bitter would be good)

1 tbsp light brown sugar

1 tbsp cocoa powder

2 tbsp chilli powder, (depending how hot you want it)

to serve:

rice

grated cheddar cheese

crusty bread

1. Heat the oil in the inner pot. Add the meat and brown.
2. Combine the rest of the ingredients with the meat and bring to the boil stirring occasionally.
3. Turn down the heat and simmer for 5 minutes with the lid on.
4. Place the inner pot into the vacuum-insulated outer Thermal container, shut the lid and leave to slow cook without power for a minimum of 2 hours.
5. Before serving, check the seasoning and adjust if necessary with salt and fresh ground pepper.
6. Serve with rice, crusty bread and a sprinkling of grated cheddar cheese.

serves: 8   minimum thermal cooking time without power: 2 hours

Pumpkin Soup with a hint of Curry
Recipe 22 - 5th November 2012

My recipe this week is Pumpkin Soup with a lovely hint of curry. It is quite thick so if you like a thinner soup you may need to add more stock.
It would make a nice soup to serve as a starter on Christmas Day.
I find a stick blender works well to blend the soup.

2 tbsp rapeseed oil

2 onions, peeled & sliced

3 cloves garlic, peeled & finely chopped

3 tbsp curry powder

2 kg pumpkin, peeled, deseeded & cut into small wedges (about 1.8kg peeled weight)

1.5 litres vegetable stock

270 ml coconut milk

1. Put the inner pot on a medium heat and add the oil.
2. When the oil is hot, add the onion, garlic and curry powder. Cook until the onions are soft.
3. Mix in the pumpkin, stir in the stock, coconut milk and crème fraîche. Bring to the boil.
4. Turn down the heat and simmer for 5 minutes with the lid on.
5. Place the inner pot into the vacuum-insulated outer Thermal Container, shut the lid and leave to slow cook without power for a minimum of 2 hours.
6. Before serving blend the contents of the inner pot, check the seasoning, adjust if necessary and bring back to the boil.
7. If you want a slightly thinner soup add a little more stock.

serves: 8   *minimum thermal cooking time with no power: 2 hours*

Christmas Pudding

Recipe 23 - 13th November 2012

Making a Christmas pudding in your thermal cooker can save a lot of fuel for all it needs is just 30 to 35 minutes simmering, then the rest of the cooking is done without power in outer container.

115 g self raising flour

115 g raisins

115 g sultanas

115 g breadcrumbs

115 g dark brown sugar

115 g vegetable shredded suet

1 large apple peeled, cored and chopped

½ tsp mixed spice

½ tsp ground cinnamon

½ tsp grated nutmeg

2 eggs

juice of a lemon

rind of a lemon

4 tbsp dark rum

250 ml milk

You will also need a 2pint or 1L pudding basin, greaseproof paper, foil and string.

1. Grease a 2 pint/1 litre pudding basin
2. Put a trivet in the inner pot. Fill with enough water to come up to 5cms below the edge of the pudding basin when placed on the trivet.
3. Bring the water in the inner pot to the boil while you add all the dry ingredients to a large mixing bowl and mix.
4. Add the eggs, lemon juice, lemon rind, rum and milk. Mix with a wooden spoon.
5. Put the mixture into the greased pudding basin.
6. Place a piece of greased, greaseproof paper on top of the mixture.
7. Cover with aluminum foil and tie round the edge, remembering to make a handle to lift the pudding out when hot.
8. Carefully place the basin in the inner pot of boiling water and bring back to the boil with the lid on.
9. Once boiling, turn down the heat and simmer for 30 minutes with the lid on.
10. Place the inner pot into the vacuum-insulated outer Thermal Container, shut the lid and leave to slow cook without power for a minimum of 5 hours.
11. Once cooked remove the pudding and allow to cool before storing for Christmas.
12. Reheat on Christmas day by placing the pudding on a trivet in the inner pot and adding water to come half way up the side of the pudding bowl. Bring to the boil, then turn the power down and simmer for 30 minutes. After 30 minutes take the inner pot off the hob and place in the Thermal Container for 2 hours or more.

serves: 8   minimum thermal cooking time without power: 5 hours

Curried Lamb Chops with Chickpeas & Spinach Recipe 24 -18th November 2012

This week to celebrate the Hindu festival Diwali I have decided to make a wonderful lamb curry in my thermal cooker.

My festive meal of curried lamb chops with chickpeas & spinach is packed with flavour, and served with basmati rice it will be the perfect dish for your family and friends.

2 tbsp ghee or vegetable oil	1 tsp cumin powder
4 bay leaves	1 tsp chilli powder
4 green cardamom pods	2 tsp garam masala
7 cloves	400 g tin chopped plum tomatoes
1 medium onion, sliced	8 small lamb chops
3 cm fresh ginger, finely grated	400 g tin of chickpeas
2 cloves garlic, finely chopped	125 g baby spinach leaves
1 tsp coriander powder	salt & pepper to taste

1. Heat the oil in the inner pot. Add the bay leaves, cardamom pods and cloves. When they sizzle, add the onion and cook until translucent and soft
2. Stir in the ginger and garlic and fry for two minutes.
3. Add the spices, tomatoes and lamb. Cover the lamb with hot water, bring to the boil and then simmer for 5 minutes.
4. Add the chickpeas and bring back to the boil and simmer for 2 to 3 minutes.
5. Turn off the heat and place the inner pot into the vacuum-insulated outer Thermal container, shut the lid. Leave while you start the rice in the top pot. If not using a top pot, leave to cook for a minimum of 2 hours.

Cooking the rice in the top pot.

1. Add the rice and water to the top pot and bring to the boil. Stir then turn down the heat and simmer for 1 minute.
2. Turn off the heat, open the vacuum-insulated outer Thermal container and place the top pot into the inner pot, put the lid on the top pot and shut the lid of the outer container.
3. Leave to thermal cook without power for a minimum of 2 hours.

Before serving

1. Check the curry for seasoning and adjust with salt and pepper if needed.
2. Add the spinach, stirring the spinach leaves into the curry until they wilt.

serves: 4   minimum thermal cooking time without power: 2 hours

Chinese Beef with Carrots
Recipe 25 - 26th November 2012

Based on a recipe by Keith Floyd from his book 'Floyd's China', Chinese Beef and Carrots' is an ideal meal to cook in a thermal cooker. I have made a few alterations to the original recipe, but it basically stays the same. Like all of my recipes, it can be made in a slow cooker, but you will not have the same energy saving as when cooking in a thermal cooker.

2 tbsp rapeseed oil	1 beef stock pot or stock cube
2 cloves garlic, peeled and finely chopped	1 tbsp light brown sugar
	3 tbsp Shaoxing rice wine (Chinese cooking wine) or dry sherry
2 slices fresh ginger root, peeled	
5 spring onions, thinly sliced	1 tsp Chinese five-spice powder
750 g stewing beef, cut into 1cm cubes	450 g carrots, cut into batons
40 ml dark soy sauce	water

1. Heat the oil in the inner pot over a medium heat.
2. Add the garlic, ginger and spring onions and cook until golden brown.
3. Add the beef and all the remaining ingredients except the water. Stir well.
4. Pour over water to cover the meat and carrots.
5. Bring to the boil and then simmer for 5 minutes.
6. Turn off the heat and place the inner pot into the vacuum-insulated outer Thermal container, shut the lid. Leave while you start the rice in the top pot. If not using a top pot leave to cook for a minimum of 3 hours.

Cooking the rice in the top pot.

1. Add the rice and water to the top pot and bring to the boil. Stir then turn down the heat and simmer for 1 minute.
2. Turn off the heat, open the vacuum-insulated outer Thermal container and place the top pot into the inner pot.
3. Put the lid on the top pot and shut the lid of the outer container.
4. Leave to thermal cook without power for a minimum of 3 hours.

Before serving

1. Check the seasoning and adjust with salt and pepper if needed
2. Serve with the rice and some stir fry vegetables.

Serves: 4   minimum thermal cooking time without power: 3 hours

Mr D's Easy Bread
Recipe 26 - 3rd December 2012

One of the most popular things to cook in a thermal cooker is bread, especially when you are far away from a place to buy some. I have over the years developed many different recipes for bread and have found this one the most reliable.

By using this as the basic bread recipe you can of course add things such as mixed seeds or cheese.

I have used a Mr D's cake tin which is specially designed to fit in the 4.5L thermal cooker.

125 g strong white bread flour, plus extra for dusting

125 g strong wholemeal flour

1 tsp salt

5 g fast-action dried yeast

¾ tbsp clear honey

175 ml warm water

butter or spread to grease the tin

1. Cut a piece of parchment (baking paper) to line the base of the bread tin.
2. Grease the tin, not forgetting the lid. Place the cut out parchment into the base.
3. Sift the flours into a large bowl and reserve the grain – the brown bits that are too big to fit through the sieve.
4. Add the salt and yeast and mix well.
5. Make a hole in the centre and pour in the honey and slightly warm water.
6. Mix well with a wooden spoon to form a smooth dough.
7. Dust your hands with flour and remove the dough. If it is not smooth, knead it until it is.
8. Shape the dough to fit the greased bread tin and place it in. Dust the top with the grain husks that you sieved earlier. Put on the lid.
9. Put a trivet in the inner pot and add 1 cup of boiling water. Place the bread tin on the trivet, put on the lid. Put the inner pot into the insulated outer container and shut the lid.
10. Leave for 45 minutes to allow the bread to rise.
11. Once risen, pour in boiling water until the water comes about ¾ of the way up the side of the bread tin.
12. Put the inner pot on a heat source and bring gently back to the boil.
13. Once boiling, turn the heat down so the water is just simmering. Do not let it boil as there is a possibility that water will get into the bread tin.
14. Simmer for 20 minutes with the inner pot lid on.
15. Turn off the heat and place the inner pot into the insulated outer container.
16. Shut the lid and leave to thermal cook without power for a minimum of four hours. It can be left overnight.
17. Once cooked, remove the tin from the inner pot and carefully take off the lid.
18. Leave for a few minutes then run a knife carefully around the edge of the bread and turn out onto a rack.

minimum thermal cooking time without power: 4 hours

Fish Tagine

Although tagines are generally meat based, fish ones are also quite common, especially in Morocco as it has the Atlantic coast which provides an abundance of fresh fish daily.
The slow cooking process of the thermal cooker mimics that of an earthenware tagine found all over North Africa. Any firm, thick fish can be used in this dish and I have even seen recipes using eels so the choice is yours.

500 g frozen line caught haddock fillets, or other sustainably caught white fish

4 tsp baharat (Middle Eastern spice mix obtainable from most large supermarkets)

1 pinch of saffron threads, soaked in 2 tbs boiling water

2 tbsp rapeseed oil

1 large onion, finely sliced

bunch of fresh coriander, leaves roughly chopped for garnish and stalks finely chopped

2 cloves garlic, crushed

80 g soft, ready-to-eat prunes, cut in half

400 g tin whole or chopped tomatoes

70 g tomato purée

4 preserved lemons, cut into small pieces

60 g green olives, stoned

For the couscous

400 g couscous

650 ml vegetable or chicken stock

1. Rub 2 tsp of baharat into the frozen fish fillets and leave to defrost.
2. Heat the oil in the inner pot over a medium-high heat, add the onion and gently cook for a few minutes until translucent.
3. Add the coriander stalks, garlic and remaining baharat and cook, stirring for 30 seconds.
4. Add the saffron, its water, the prunes, tomatoes, tomato purée and 500ml of water.
5. Bring to the boil stirring occasionally.
6. Turn down the heat and simmer for 5 minutes.
7. Add the defrosted fish and all the baharat you used as the rub. Bring back to the boil.
8. Turn off the heat and place the inner pot into the insulated outer container.
9. Shut the lid and leave to thermal cook without power for a minimum of one hour.
10. Serve with some nicely steamed vegetables.

Cooking the couscous in the top pot

1. Place the couscous in the top pot.
2. Pour the stock over, stir and bring to the boil.
3. Turn off the heat, open the vacuum-insulated outer Thermal container and place the top pot into the inner pot.
4. Put the lid on the top pot and shut the lid of the outer container.
5. Leave to thermal cook without power for a minimum of 1 hour.

Serving

1. Gently break up the fish with two forks.
2. Serve on the couscous with a scatter of the roughly chopped coriander.

serves: 4   *minimum thermal cooking time without power: 1 hour*

Venison and Wild Rice
Recipe 28 - 18th December 2012

The inspiration for the dish came from a cookbook "Stories and Recipes of the Great Depression of the 1930's". I did a little modification of it for the thermal cooker and found it was a very tasty dish. If you wanted to use beef instead of venison I am sure that it would work just as well.

Rice
1 cup of wild rice

1.5 cups of water

Venison
2 tbsp rapeseed oil

200 g smoked lardons

1 medium onion, sliced

500 g venison, cubed

1 green pepper, roughly chopped

300 g potatoes, cubed

1 tsp chilli powder

1 tsp curry powder

400 g tomatoes, chopped

200 ml water

1 tsp salt

1 tsp freshly ground pepper

Cooking the wild rice
1. Place the rice in a pan, add the water, bring to the boil and boil for 3 minutes.
2. Take off the heat, put on a lid and leave for later.

Cooking the venison
1. Heat the oil in the inner pot over a medium-high heat, add the lardons and cook for a couple of minutes.
2. Add the onion and cook until it softens.
3. Add the venison and cook until it colours.
4. Stir in the green pepper, potatoes, chilli powder and curry powder.
5. Add the tin of tomatoes, water, salt and pepper.
6. Bring to the boil, stirring occasionally.
7. Turn down the heat and simmer for 5 minutes.

8. Drain the rice and stir it into the venison.

9. Bring back to the boil.

10. Turn off the heat and place the inner pot into the insulated outer container.

11. Shut the lid and leave to thermal cook without power for a minimum of three hours.

12. Serve with some nicely steamed vegetables.

serves: 4   *minimum thermal cooking time without power: 3 hours*

The Best Venison Chilli
Recipe 29 - 15th January 2013

My venison chilli recipe, cooked in a thermal cooker or crock-pot is an easy recipe and can be made for supper any day of the week. Chilli tastes so much better if left to slowly cook so please don't rush this one.

If you don't want to use venison you could use beef/chicken/pork or for a vegetarian version you could substitute the meat for a selection of different beans and use a vegetable stock cube. I however put venison the top of my favourite chilli list and it is certainly worth trying.

You should be able to get venison mince from your butcher, but if you have problems you can purchase it on line. In the recipe I have used tinned kidney beans, but if you would prefer to use dried, remember to soak them overnight before boiling for about 20 minutes to make sure you remove any toxins which can make you ill.

Serve the thermally cooked chilli on a bed of rice and topped with sour cream or grated cheddar cheese and you will have the ultimate comfort food.

Rice

2 cups of rice

3 cups of water

Chilli

2 tbsp rapeseed oil

2 medium onions, chopped

1 small chilli, finely chopped

2 cloves garlic, crushed

200 g chopped smoked bacon pieces

500 g minced venison

1 tbsp ground cumin

1 tbsp ground coriander

2 tsp smoked paprika

400 g tin of chopped tomatoes

70 g tomato purée

200 ml water

1 beef stock cube

400 g tin kidney beans, drained

salt and pepper

1. Heat the rapeseed oil in the inner pot over a medium-high heat and add the bacon pieces and cook until they start to crisp slightly.
2. Add the onion, chilli and garlic. Cook until the onion softens.
3. Add the venison and cook until it colours.
4. Stir in the cumin, coriander and smoked paprika and cook for 1 minute.
5. Add the tin of tomatoes, tomato purée, water, stock cube and kidney beans.
6. Bring to the boil, stirring occasionally.
7. Turn down the heat and simmer for 5 minutes.
8. Turn off the heat and place the inner pot into the vacuum-insulated outer Thermal container.
9. Shut the lid and leave while you start the rice in the top pot. If not using a top pot, leave to cook for a minimum of 2 hours.

Cooking the rice in the top pot

1. Add the rice and water to the top pot and bring to the boil, stir and turn down the heat and simmer for 1 minute.
2. Turn off the heat, open the vacuum-insulated outer Thermal container and place the top pot into the inner pot.
3. Put the lid on the top pot and shut the lid of the outer container.
4. Leave to thermal cook without power for a minimum of 2 hours.

To serve

Serve the chilli on a bed of rice with a spoonful of sour cream or grated cheddar cheese on top.

serves: 4   minimum thermal cooking time without power: 2 hours

Lamb with Rosemary & Sweet Potatoes

Recipe 30 - 23rd January 2013

Lamb and rosemary as we all know are great partners but by adding sweet potatoes, they make this dish the perfect lamb casserole to cook in your thermal cooker.

This recipe is available as a video at YouTube.com/MrDsKitchen so if you want to see how simple it is why not watch my step-by-step video.

2 tbsp rapeseed oil

450 g lamb shoulder, cut into 2 cm cubes

1 large onion, cut into thin wedges

500 ml beef stock

2 tbsp beef gravy granules

450 g sweet potatoes, peeled and cut into 2 cm cubes

200 g French beans, cut into short lengths

1 tsp dried rosemary

2 bay leaves

salt and freshly ground black pepper

to serve:

mashed potatoes or crusty bread.

1. Heat the rapeseed oil in the inner pot over a medium-high heat and add the lamb
2. Brown the lamb.
3. Add all the other ingredients and bring to the boil, stirring occasionally.
4. Turn down the heat and simmer for 5 minutes.
5. Turn off the heat and place the inner pot into the vacuum-insulated outer Thermal container.
6. Shut the lid and leave for a minimum of 2 hours.

To serve

1. Check for seasoning and add salt and pepper if necessary.
2. Serve with creamy mashed potatoes or crusty bread.

serves: 4   minimum thermal cooking time without power: 2 hours

Pheasant Chinese Style

Recipe 31 - 29th January 2013

The Pheasant is native to Asia, so it seemed right to make a Chinese dish adapted from a recipe by Hank Shaw, using a pheasant from our local farm shop. This recipe is available as a video at YouTube.com/MrDsKitchen so why not watch my step-by-step video.

1 whole pheasant

500 ml water

1 chicken stock pot or stock cube

6 cm ginger root, peeled and cut in half

6 spring onions, sliced on an angle

3 star anise

1 chilli, finely sliced (remove the seeds if you don't want it too hot)

100 g fresh shiitake mushrooms, thinly sliced

4 tbsp peanut oil

1 tsp Sichuan peppercorns

2 tbsp Shaoxing wine or dry sherry

3 tbsp rice vinegar

1 tsp potato or corn starch mixed with 1 tbsp. cold water

1 tbsp. sesame oil

Salt

Rice   1 cup rice

2 cups water

1. Put the water and chicken stock into the inner pot and bring to the boil, stirring to dissolve the stock pot.

2. Add all the other ingredients except the pheasant, bring back to the boil.

3. Put in the pheasant, top up with water to cover the bird and bring back to the boil.

4. Turn down the heat and simmer for 5 minutes.

5. Turn off the heat and place the inner pot into the outer Thermal container.

6. Shut the lid and leave for a minimum of 2.5 hours.

Cooking the rice in the top pot.

1. Add the rice and water to the top pot, bring to the boil, stir, then turn down the heat and simmer for 1 minute.

2. Turn off the heat, open the outer Thermal container, place the top pot into the inner pot, put the lid on the top pot and shut the lid of the outer container.

3. Leave to thermal cook without power for the same time as main meal.

To serve   Add salt and pepper if necessary. Shred the meat off the pheasant and put it on a bed of rice. Serve with some stir fried vegetables.

serves: 2   minimum thermal cooking time without power: 2hrs 30mins

Chinese Oxtail Stew

Recipe 32 - 5th February 2013

Over two years ago I made a video of this recipe, "Chinese Oxtail Stew" and it has become the most popular video on YouTube.com/MrDsKitchen..
The video has had over 15,500 viewings so to celebrate the start of the Chinese New Year of the Snake I have decided to do a written version of the recipe.

Oxtail tends no longer to come from an ox, instead it now mainly comes from a cow.

The tail is skinned and cut into sections. Each section has some marrow in the centre and a bony portion of meat surrounding it. The meat, which needs long slow cooking, is gelatinous, and is best used for stocks and soups making it an ideal meat to cook in a thermal cooker.

2 tbsp rapeseed oil

1 oxtail cut into pieces

250 ml Shaoxing wine or dry sherry

180 ml dark soy sauce

1 litre water

1 large cube of yellow rock sugar (from Chinese supermarket) or 2 tbsp brown sugar

2 star anise

2 cloves garlic, crushed

6 to 8 slices ginger root, 1cm thick

6 strips orange peel

to serve

2 cups rice

3 cups water

1 tsp salt

1. Heat the oil in the inner pot, add the oxtail and brown on all sides, then remove and put it to one side for later.
2. Pour off any excess fat from the inner pot and put back on the heat.
3. Add the Shaoxing wine and stir to deglaze the pot by scraping off all the browned bits that have stuck to the bottom. These deglazed browned bits are loaded with flavour.
4. Add all the other ingredients and bring to the boil whilst stirring to melt the sugar.
6 Once the sugar has melted, put the browned oxtail in the pot, bring back to the boil, then turn down the heat and simmer for 10 minutes.
5. Turn off the heat and place the inner pot into the outer Thermal container.
6. Shut the lid and leave for a minimum of 4 hours.

If cooking the rice in the top pot.

1. Add the rice, water and salt to the top pot, bring to the boil, stir, then turn down the heat and simmer for 1 minute.
2. Turn off the heat, open the vacuum-insulated outer Thermal container and place the top pot into the inner pot.
3. Put the lid on the top pot and shut the lid of the outer container.
4. Leave to thermal cook without power for the same time as main meal.

To serve

1. Check for seasoning and add salt and pepper if necessary.
2. Serve the oxtail on a bed of rice with stir fried pak choi.

serves: 2 - 4   *minimum thermal cooking time without power: 4 hours*

Kerala Fish Curry

Recipe 33 - 13th February 2013

Kerala's long coastline with its numerous rivers and backwaters has contributed to many sea and river food dishes to be found in this region of India.

This curry is typical of the type you will find in Kerala, being served in both small and large restaurants. Due to the weather, the selection of spices available in South India are vast and I have included some of the more popular ones in this dish.

The beautiful yellow colour is created using turmeric, which has been used in India for thousands of years and is a major part of certain types of traditional Indian medicine.

Coconut milk, which forms the base of the dish, is widely used in Kerala for thickening and flavour and comes from the coconuts which grow in abundance.

Just like any other recipe, each chef will have their own variation and this is mine for Kerala Fish Curry.

2 tbsp ghee or vegetable oil

½ tsp black mustard seeds

½ tsp cumin seeds

½ tsp ground turmeric

1 medium onion, finely chopped

1 clove garlic, finely chopped

2.5 cm ginger root, finely chopped

1 green chilli, finely chopped (remove seeds if you don't want it too hot)

10 curry leaves

400 ml can coconut milk

400 ml water

1 fish stock cube

400 g tin of chopped tomatoes

500 g firm fish (you could use salmon if you wish)

to serve   2 cups rice and 3 cups water

1. Put the ghee or oil in the inner pot over a medium heat, add the mustard seeds, cumin seeds and turmeric. When the seeds start to pop add the onion, garlic and ginger.
2. Cook gently for about 5 minutes until the onion is translucent, then add the curry leaves and chilli. Cook for 5 more minutes.
3. Pour in the coconut milk and water. Crumble in the stock cube before adding the tin of tomatoes. Stir well to dissolve the stock cube.
4. Check the seasoning, add some salt if necessary, bring to the boil and then turn down the heat and simmer for 5 minutes.
5. Add the fish, bring it back to the boil, then turn off the heat and place the inner pot into the vacuum-insulated outer Thermal container.
6. Shut the lid and leave for a minimum of 1 hour.

NOTE: If you want to wait longer for your food than this, do everything except adding the fish, which you can add about 30 minutes before serving by bringing the curry sauce back to the boil, adding the fish and then putting the inner pot back into the outer container to finish cooking.

Cooking the rice in Mr D's Top Pot

1. Add the rice and water to the top pot, bring to the boil, stir, then turn down the heat and simmer for 1 minute.
2. Turn off the heat, open the outer Thermal container and place the top pot into the inner pot. Put the lid on the top pot and shut the lid of the outer container.
3. Leave to thermal cook without power for the same time as main meal

serves: 2 - 3   *minimum thermal cooking time without power: 1 hour*

Rajasthan Lamb Chops
Recipe 34 - 20th February 2013

Much of the best Indian cuisine has derived from the Mughals. They, along with the Europeans, influenced many of the royal kitchens of India.
In Rajasthan though, the common man's kitchen remained untouched and the cooking was influenced by the war-like lifestyle of its inhabitants and the availability of ingredients in this region.
The food of Rajasthan has its own unique flavour and the simplest ingredients go into preparing most dishes.

850 g lamb chops (8 chops)

Marinade **4 tbsp yoghurt**

         2 tbsp turmeric, ground

         2 tsp salt

The curry **2 tbsp. vegetable oil**

         2 medium onions, thinly sliced

         3 cloves garlic, chopped

         2 cm fresh ginger root, chopped

         1 tbsp cumin seeds

         1 tbsp coriander seeds

         1 tbsp fennel seeds

         ½ tsp chilli flakes

         1 tsp salt

         400 g tin chopped tomatoes

1. Mix together the marinade and coat the chops with it.
2. Put in the fridge for a minimum of 1 hour.
3. Grind the garlic and ginger to become a paste.
4. Dry roast the cumin seeds, coriander seeds, fennel seeds and chilli flakes in a frying pan until aromatic and just starting to change colour.
5. Remove from the heat and grind using a spice grinder or pestle & mortar into a fine powder. Set aside.
6. Put the inner pot onto a medium heat and add the oil.
7. Add the onions and fry until just starting to brown.
8. Add the garlic/ginger paste and cook for 1 minute, then add the ground spices and cook for another minute while stirring.

9. Pour in the tin of tomatoes and then add the chops and any remaining marinade.

10. Bring to the boil.

11. Turn down the heat and simmer for 10 minutes.

12. Turn off the heat and place the inner pot into the vacuum-insulated outer Thermal container.

13. Shut the lid and leave for a minimum of 3 hours.

To serve

1. Check for seasoning and add salt and pepper if necessary.

2. Serve the lamb chops with rice and naan bread.

serves: 2 - 4   minimum thermal cooking time without power: 3 hours

51

Sausage Casserole

The humble sausage can make a cheap and delicious meal.

It is always worth buying a good quality sausage with a high meat content.

In this recipe you can use pork, beef or maybe venison, the choice is yours. The mung beans add a lovely note of flavour.

This meal can be served with crusty bread or leave the potatoes out and cook them in a top pot and then mash them before serving.

1 tbsp olive oil

2 large onions, peeled and sliced

1 clove garlic, crushed

8 sausages of your choice

2 carrots peeled and sliced

400 g tin mung beans

200 g frozen peas

2 celery stalks washed and sliced thinly

3 large floury potatoes peeled (these can be cooked separately in a top pot if you would like to serve as mashed potato)

2 tbsp Lea and Perrin Worcestershire sauce

1 beef stock cube

250 ml red wine

400 g tin tomatoes, chopped

150 ml of water

1 tsp dried herbs

Salt and pepper to season

1. Heat the oil in the inner pot and add the onions.
2. Add the garlic and fry the onions until they are golden brown.
3. Remove the onions and add the sausages. Brown the sausages.
4. Replace the onions and all of the other ingredients.
5. Put on the lid and bring to the boil.
6. Reduce the heat down to a simmer and cook for 5 minutes.
7. Turn off the heat and place the inner pot into the vacuum-insulated outer Thermal Container.
8. Shut the lid and leave for a minimum of 2 hours.

To serve

1. Check for seasoning and add salt and pepper if necessary.
2. Serve with crusty bread

serves: 2   *minimum thermal cooking time without power: 2 hours*

Chicken Stew

Recipe 36 - 5th March 2013

This week's recipe is adapted from one by Sarah Buenfield that appeared in the Good Food Magazine.

Once you have done the initial preparation, this one pot dish can be put together with the smallest amount of work and the long slow cooking in your thermal cooker makes a wonderfully flavoursome meal.

I served the chicken stew with new potatoes but it would be perfect with mash to mop up the lovely sauce the slow cooking makes.

1 tbsp rapeseed oil

1 medium onion , finely chopped

2 cloves garlic, sliced

1.5 litres hot water

2 chicken stock cubes or stock pots

1 large potato, finely grated

1 tbsp fresh thyme leaves

2 tsp fresh rosemary leaves

8 chicken thighs

4 chicken legs

6 carrots , cut into chunks

2 parsnips , cut into chunks

3 leeks , well washed and thickly sliced

salt and pepper to taste

to serve

1. Heat the oil in the inner pot.
2. Add the onion and garlic and fry for a few minutes until soft
3. Pour in the water and add the stock cubes. Bring to the boil, stirring occasionally to dissolve the stock cubes
4. Add the potato and herbs and chicken and bring back to the boil.
5. Stir in the carrots, parsnips and leeks.
6. Put on the lid and bring to the boil.
7. Reduce the heat down to a simmer and cook for 5 minutes.
8. Turn off the heat and place the inner pot into the vacuum-insulated outer Thermal Container.
9. Shut the lid and leave for a minimum of 2 hours.

To serve

1 . Check for seasoning and add salt and pepper if necessary.

2 . Serve with mashed potatoes.

serves: 4   *minimum thermal cooking time without power: 2 hours*

Navarin of Coley

Recipe 37 - 12th March 2013

Navarin is normally French ragoût (stew) of lamb or mutton. Often, vegetables are added, and the name "navarin" has been suggested to relate to the 1827 Battle of Navarino.

In this recipe I am using fish instead of meat for the stew, and the vegetables are broad beans, carrots and courgettes. The fish I am using is coley but you could use sustainable cod or even monkfish if you prefer.

25 g butter

2 tbsp rapeseed oil

175 g fresh or frozen baby broad beans

1 medium onion, sliced

225 g baby carrots, trimmed and halved lengthways

225 g courgettes, cut into chunks

1 clove garlic, crushed

4 tbsp plain flour

200 ml white wine

300 ml water

1 fish stock cube or stock pot

1 tbsp lemon juice

3 tbsp crème fraîche

2 tbsp flat leaf parsley, chopped

1 kg thick coley fillet, skinned and cut into 3 to 4cm cubes

salt and pepper

to serve

new potatoes

1. Heat the butter and oil in the inner pot.
2. Add the broad beans, onion, carrots, courgettes and garlic and fry for a few minutes until the onion softens.
3. Stir in the flour and mix until it forms a roux
4. Pour in the wine, stirring all the time to avoid lumps.
5. Add the water and stock cube. Stir until the stock cube is dissolved.
6. Stir in the lemon juice, then the crème fraîche and parsley. Bring to the boil.
7. Add the fish and then turn off the heat.
8. Put on the lid and place the inner pot into the outer Thermal Container.
9. Shut the lid and leave for a minimum of 1 hour.

To serve

1. Check for seasoning and add salt and pepper if necessary.
2. Serve with new potatoes.

serves: 3   minimum thermal cooking time without power: 1 hour

54

Pigeon Casserole

Recipe 38 - 20th March 2013

This recipe is adapted from the CookitSimple website. I made it the other day while packing for the Bath Motorhome and Caravan Show. On arrival at the show we set up our stand and then served it later in our caravan, for our evening meal. One pigeon per person cooked slowly in red wine and served on a bed of diced onions and carrots with new potatoes and fresh vegetables makes a great meal.

I bought my pigeons at our local farm shop, but you can also buy them online.

30 g butter

130 g pancetta, diced

4 pigeons or 2 wood pigeons

2 large onions, skinned and chopped

4 medium carrots, peeled and chopped

2 bay leaves

2 tsp fresh parsley, chopped

1 tsp dried thyme

1 tsp freshly ground black pepper

2 tbsp plain flour

750 ml beef stock

250 ml red wine

salt

to serve

new potatoes or mash

fresh vegetables of your choice

1. Melt the butter in the inner pot over a medium heat, add the pancetta and fry for 2 minutes
2. Add the pigeons 2 at a time and brown all over.
3. Remove the pigeons and add the chopped onions and carrots and cook until the onions soften.
4. Add the freshly ground pepper and flour, mix well, replace the pigeons and pour over the red wine and stock. Stir well.
5. Bring to the boil skimming off any impurities, and then turn down the heat and simmer for 5 minutes.
6. Put on the lid and place the inner pot into the outer Thermal Container.
7. Shut the lid and leave for a minimum of 4 hours.

To serve

1. Check for seasoning and add salt if necessary.
2. Serve 1 pigeon per person on a bed of the onions and carrots with new potatoes and fresh vegetables

serves: 4   minimum thermal cooking time without power: 4 hours

Paella de Marisco with Salmon & Prawn
Recipe 39 - 27th March 2013

There are three widely known types of paella:

Paella Valenciana - consists of white rice, green vegetables, meat (rabbit, chicken, duck), land snails, beans and seasoning.

Paella de Marisco - replaces meat and snails with seafood and omits beans and green vegetables.

Paella Mixta - is a free-style combination of meat, seafood, vegetables, and sometimes beans.

This recipe uses seafood but you could easily change to meat or vegetarian by using the same base and replacing the seafood with whatever you wish.

1 tbsp rapeseed oil

1 medium onion, chopped

2 cloves garlic, crushed

186 g rice

1 tsp crushed chillies

1 tsp smoked paprika

1 pinch saffron

600 ml fish stock

1 green pepper, de-seeded and chopped

200 g tin chopped tomatoes

1 tsp salt

100 g frozen peas, thawed

75 g sweet corn

175 g peeled prawns

450 g salmon, cut into cubes

to serve

1 lemon, cut into wedges

1. Put the oil in the inner pot over a medium heat.
2. Add the onion and garlic and cook until the the onions soften.
3. Add the rice and saffron. Stir to make sure the rice is mixed well with the oil, onions and garlic.
4. Add everything else except the peas, sweetcorn, prawns and salmon. Bring to the boil.
5. Turn down the heat and simmer for 3 minutes.
6. Mix in the peas, sweetcorn, prawns and salmon. Bring back to the boil.
7. Turn down the heat and simmer for 2 minutes.
8. If you have a top pot, place this in the inner pot and fill with boiling water*.
9. Place the inner pot into the vacuum-insulated outer Thermal Container.
10. Shut the lid and leave for a minimum of 1 hour.

To serve

Serve with lemon wedges.

* This dish will best if only cooked for a maximum of 2 hours, but can be left longer where the volume of hot ingredients is increased by placing a top pot filled with boiling water into the inner pot.

serves: 2   *minimum thermal cooking time without power: 1 hour*

Malaysian Meatball Curry

Recipe 40 - 3rd April 2013

I just love Malaysian curry and this one is very versatile.

Although I have made this with beef meatballs you can add whatever meat you prefer.

For this meal you will need to either buy or make up your own Malaysian curry powder. I have listed the ingredients to make your own, and any unused curry powder can be stored in a sealed container until needed again. Like all spices, to get the best flavour, you should not keep it too long.

Ingredients for Curry Powder (grind in a grinder)

2 tbsp coriander seeds

1 tbsp cumin seed

¾ tbsp fennel seed

½ tbsp chili powder

½ tsp turmeric

¼ tsp cloves

¼ tsp cinnamon

¼ tsp cardamom

¼ tsp black pepper

To serve (with rice cooked in top pot)

2 cups rice

3 cups water

Ingredients for Curry

2 tbsp rapeseed oil

3 large onions, sliced

2 cloves garlic, chopped

2 cm fresh ginger, sliced

5 tbsp Malaysian meat curry powder (see above)

1 tsp chili powder, or to taste

12 small beef meatballs (I used ready made but you can make your own)

400 g tin coconut milk

500 ml water

2 star anise

8 curry leaves

2 medium potatoes, cut into chunks

4 tbsp tomato paste

3 tbsp finely chopped coriander

salt and pepper

1. Heat the oil in the inner pot over a low heat.
2. Add the onions, garlic and ginger. Fry on a low heat until the onions are soft.
3. Stir in the Malaysian curry powder and chilli powder. Cook for 2 minutes, making sure it doesn't burn.
4. Turn up the heat to medium and add the meatballs. Make sure they are nicely covered by the curry mixture and cook until they brown. You may need to add a little more oil but don't add too much.
5. Remove the meatballs and keep on a plate.

6. Add the coconut milk, star anise and curry leaves. Slowly bring to a boil.
7. Carefully add the meatballs back into the inner pot, stirring occasionally.
8. Add the potatoes, bring back to the boil and boil for 5 minutes uncovered, then add tomato paste, season with salt and stir gently to mix.
9. Put on the lid, turn off the heat and place the inner pot into the vacuum-insulated outer Thermal Container.
10. Shut the lid and leave to cook for a minimum of 2 hours.
11. When ready to serve, stir in the coriander. Check the seasoning and adjust if necessary.

To serve

Serve with bread or steamed rice.

serves: 2   minimum thermal cooking time without power: 2 hours

Upside Down Pudding

Recipe 41 - 10th April 2013

This classic retro pineapple upside-down cake is so easy to make in a thermal cooker.

For this recipe I have used the Mr D's Cake Tin and trivet but you could use and cake tin that will fit in your thermal cooker. Remember though to make a lid to cover the cake tin so that condensation does not fall on the pudding while it is cooking.

Ingredients for topping

3 tbsp honey

227 g tin pineapples rings in syrup, drained

100 g glacé cherries

Ingredients for the cake

100 g plain flour

1 tsp baking powder

¼ tsp bicarbonate of soda

100 g soft butter

100 g caster sugar

2 medium eggs

to serve

ice cream or double cream

1. Drizzle a layer of honey in the base of the Mr D's Cake Tin.
2. Arrange the pineapple slices as in the picture.
3. Fill each pineapple ring with a glace cherry.
4. Put the flour, baking powder, bicarbonate of soda, butter, caster sugar and eggs into a bowl and mix until smooth.
5. Add 3 tablespoons of pineapple juice to thin it a little.
6. Pour this mixture carefully over the cherry-studded pineapple rings and spread it out gently.
7. Put the lid on the cake tin and place it in the inner pot on a trivet.
8. Carefully pour boiling down the side of the cake tin until comes ¾ of the way up the side of the tin.
9. Put on the inner pot lid and bring back to the boil. Once boiling, turn down the heat and simmer for 12 minutes.

10. Turn off the heat and place the inner pot into the vacuum-insulated outer Thermal Container.

11. Shut the lid and leave to cook for a minimum of 3 to 4 hours.

12 When ready carefully remove the cake tin and remove the lid. Leave for a few minutes before running a knife around the side of the pudding and turning it out onto a plate.

To serve

Serve warm with ice cream or double cream.

serves: 3 - 4   minimum thermal cooking time without power: 3 hours

Lamb Pulao
Recipe 42 - 17th April 2013

Many people think that a biryani and a pulao are the same thing especially as they look very much the same as they are both rice based but there are a number of differences.

Layering – when making a biryani, the rice is normally cooked separately and it is layered with meat or vegetables cooked in a masala (a mixture of spices and other ingredients). In a pulao, the ingredients are not layered. The rice is sautéed with other ingredients and cooked together.

Strength of Spice – a biryani is normally much heavier in spices including chilli powder, garlic, ginger, and green chillies than a pulao. A pulao on the other hand does not include as large a volume of these ingredients and will also balance the spices with other ingredients like dried raisins and nuts.

One pot preparation – pulaos are generally easier to make in a thermal cooker as they're mainly completed in a single pot and don't call for the separate cooking and ultimate pairing and stacking of rice and meat masala like a biryani does.

Ingredients

350 g basmati rice

175 g ghee

2 medium onions, chopped

2 cloves garlic, crushed

8 cloves

12 black peppercorns

5 cm cinnamon stick

5 green cardamom pods

750 g lamb or mutton, cut into 2.5 cm cubes

1 tsp salt

900 ml lamb stock

225 g small potatoes, cut in half if more than 5 cm in length

2 tbsp natural yogurt

15 g ginger, crushed

1 tbsp tomato purée

1 tsp cumin seeds

1 tsp chilli powder

½ tsp ground cinnamon

to serve

1 tomato, thinly sliced

100 g cashew nuts

1. Soak the rice in water for 30 minutes then drain.
2. Heat the ghee to the inner pot and fry the onions, garlic, cloves, peppercorns, cinnamon stick and cardamom pods until the onions are golden brown.
3. Remove a small amount of the onions for garnish then add the meat, 1 teaspoon of salt and the stock and bring to the boil.
4. Turn down the heat and simmer for 5 minutes.
5. Add the potatoes and bring back to the boil and simmer for another 5 minutes.
6. Stir in the yogurt, ginger, tomato purée and the rest of the spices.
7. Mix in the rice.
8. Bring back to the boil and boil for 2 minutes.
9. Turn off the heat and place the inner pot into the vacuum-insulated outer Thermal Container.
10. Shut the lid and leave to cook for a minimum of 3 hours.

To serve

Serve garnished with the reserved fried onions, thin slices of tomatoes and cashew nuts sprinkled over the top.

serves: 4 - 6   minimum thermal cooking time without power: 3 hours

Kedgeree
Recipe 43 - 24th April 2013

Following a request at the motorhome show in Peterborough, I created this recipe for kedgeree in my thermal cooker.

Kedgeree was a breakfast dish in the time of the Raj but now is eaten at any time of the day. The fish and hard boiled eggs were a British introduction and Lizzie Collingham points out in 'Curry: a biography' that fresh fish was already a staple of the Raj breakfast table as "in the hot season, fish caught early in the morning would be much deteriorated before the dinner hour."

When the dish was brought back to the country houses of Britain, smoked haddock started being used, but you can use any type of fish you prefer.

2 medium hard-boiled eggs, peeled and cut into quarters

1 tbsp rapeseed oil

100 g butter

1 large onion, finely sliced

1 green chilli, deseeded and cut into thin rings

1 tbsp Madras curry powder

3 crushed cardamom pods

3 cups Basmati rice

4½ cups water

fish stock cube

½ lemon, juice extracted

500 g smoked haddock

to serve

Small bunch of coriander, chopped

1. Heat the oil and butter in the inner pot, fry the onions until soft, then stir in the curry powder, chili and cardamom pods. Cook for 2 minutes.
2. Add the rice and stir well until it is mixed with the onions and curry powder.
3. Add the water, stock cube and lemon juice. Stirring from time to time, bring to the boil, then turn down the heat, and simmer for 5 minutes.
4. Place the fish on the top of the rice skin side down and put on the inner pot lid.
5. Turn off the heat, place the inner pot into the outer Thermal Container, shut the lid and leave to thermally cook without power for a minimum of 2 hours.

To serve

1. Remove the skin from the fish and flake it into the rice.
2. Check the seasoning and adjust if needed.
3. Serve with the eggs on top of the kedgeree and garnished with the coriander.

serves: 4   *minimum thermal cooking time without power: 2 hours*

Caribbean Chicken

Recipe 44 - 30th April 2013

This Caribbean Chicken recipe is such an easy dish to prepare in a thermal cooker. The dish has a wonderful mixture of flavours and textures that you will love.
If you want to serve more people you can easily increase the amount by multiply up the ingredients.

450 g chicken thighs, boned and each thigh cut into three

300 ml of chicken stock

400 g black beans, drained and rinsed

225 g tomato and garlic sauce

1 medium onion, roughly chopped

1 green pepper, roughly chopped

½ tsp ground cinnamon

¼ tsp ground cloves

1 tsp cayenne pepper

4 tbsp white rum

1 ½ cups rice

salt & pepper

1. Put all the ingredients in the inner pot.
2. Bring to the boil with the lid on.
3. Turn down the heat and simmer for 5 minutes.
4. Turn off the heat and place the inner pot into the vacuum-insulated outer Thermal Container.
5. Shut the lid and leave to thermally cook without power for a minimum of 2 hours.

Cooking the rice in the top pot

1. Add the rice and three cups of water to the top pot and bring to the boil, stir and turn down the heat and simmer for 1 minute.
2. Turn off the heat, open the vacuum-insulated Thermal Container and remove the lid from the inner container. Place the top pot into the inner pot.
3. Leave to thermal cook without power for the same length of time as the Caribbean Chicken.

To serve

Before serving check the seasoning and adjust if necessary.

serves: 2   minimum thermal cooking time without power: 2 hours

Rhubarb Marmalade

Recipe 45 - 8th May 2013

The original recipe came from 'The Fireless Cookbook', written around 1900.

I have used this method to make orange marmalade in the past and it can be very easily adapted to any jam or marmalade. Although it may seem a very long winded way to make jams and marmalades, it is certainly a way to save fuel.

170 g rhubarb, chopped into 2 to 3 cm lengths

3 pieces stem ginger, chopped

2 medium oranges, juice extracted and the skin cut into thin strips

1 lemon, juice extracted

1.2 kg jam sugar

small lump of butter to remove scum at setting point

1. Put the chopped rhubarb, chopped stem ginger, sliced orange peel, lemon and orange juice in the inner pot and bring to the boil, stirring occasionally to stop it catching.

2. Turn down the heat and simmer for 5 minutes, stirring occasionally, then put on the lid, turn off the heat, place the inner pot into the outer Thermal Container, shut the lid and leave to thermally cook without power for a minimum of 10 hours.

3. Remove the inner pot and bring back to the boil, stirring occasionally, then once again place the inner pot into the vacuum-insulated outer Thermal Container, shut the lid and leave to thermally cook without power for another 10 hours.

4. Remove the inner pot, add the sugar and bring to the boil while stirring to dissolve the sugar. When completely dissolved, turn off the heat, place the inner pot into the outer Thermal Container, shut the lid and leave to thermally cook without power for the final 10 hours.

5. Remove the inner pot and bring up to jam setting temperature (104°C or 222°F). Don't worry about the scum that can form on the surface at this stage.

6. Test for a set by placing a teaspoonful of the marmalade on to a chilled saucer. Let it cool in the fridge, then push it with your finger: if a crinkly skin has formed on the jam, then it has set. It if hasn't, boil for another 5 minutes, then do another test.

7. When setting, turn off the heat, stir in the small lump of butter (to remove the scum) and leave for 15 minutes before bottling into sterilized hot jars, filling them as near to the top as possible.

8. Place a waxed disc over the surface, then seal with a lid.

minimum thermal cooking time without power: 30 hours

Pork Sausages and Herbs
Recipe 46 - 15th May 2013

Another really tasty dish and so easy to make in your motorhome, caravan or tent.

You could easily make a vegetarian version using vegetarian sausages and vegetable stock.

I have used small casserole free range sausages but if you are using normal sized sausages, they should be cut in half.

2 tbsp rapeseed oil

500 g good quality casserole pork sausages. If using normal sized, cut in half

2 medium red onions, chopped

500 g potatoes, diced

250 g carrots, diced

400 g tin chopped tomatoes

1 chicken stock pot or cube

500 ml water

1 tsp dried thyme

1 tsp dried sage

½ tsp freshly ground pepper

salt

1. Put 1 tablespoon of the oil in the inner pot over a medium heat
2. Add the sausages and fry until they start to brown.
3. Remove the sausages and keep on a plate to add later.
4. Add the remaining oil, potatoes and carrots and fry for 3 minutes, stirring from time to time. If the vegetables start to stick, add a small dash of water.
5. Add all the other ingredients except the salt and bring to the boil.
6. Place the sausages back in the inner pot and bring back to the boil.
7. Once boiling, put on the lid turn down the heat and simmer for 5 minutes.
8. Give the casserole a stir before turning off the heat and placing the inner pot into the vacuum-insulated outer Thermal Container.
9. Shut the lid and leave to thermally cook without power for a minimum of 2 hours.
10. Before serving, check the seasoning and adjust if necessary.
11. Serve with greens of your choice

serves: 4   minimum thermal cooking time without power: 2 hours

Beans & Mushroom Hotpot

Recipe 47 - 23rd May 2013

This recipe for National Vegetarian Week is a classic to which I have given a little bit of a twist by using chunky bean soup. I bought mine from Waitrose, but any bean soup will be fine.

National Vegetarian Week, usually in May, sets out to prove that among other things vegetarian food can be delicious and not only for non-meat eaters.

3 tbsp rapeseed oil

500 g chestnut mushrooms, chopped

200 g small button mushrooms

1 large onion, chopped

2 tbsp Madras curry powder

125 ml dry white wine

400 g tin of tomatoes, chopped

2 tbsp sun-dried tomato paste

2 x 400 g tins chunky mixed bean soup

3 tbsp mango chutney

60 ml mint leaves, roughly chopped (¼ cup)

60 ml coriander. roughly chopped (¼ cup)

1. Heat the oil in the inner pot over medium-low heat
2. Add the onions and mushrooms. Cook until the onions are soft.
3. Stir in the curry powder and wine. Cook for 2 minutes.
4. Add the tomatoes, sun-dried tomato paste and tins of soup. Bring to the boil, stirring occasionally.
5. Stir in the mango chutney and mint.
6. Turn down the heat and simmer for 5 minutes.
7. Give the casserole a stir before turning off the heat and placing the inner pot into the vacuum-insulated outer Thermal Container.
8. Shut the lid and leave to thermally cook without power for a minimum of 1 hour.
9. Before serving, check the seasoning and adjust if necessary.
10 Garnish with the fresh coriander leaves and serve with a crusty roll.

serves: 4   *minimum thermal cooking time without power: 1 hour*

Mediterranean Squid with Couscous
Recipe 48 - 29th May 2013

Although stir-frying is a good quick way to cook squid, a gentle slow cooking in red wine flavoured with garlic and thyme will make the squid a delicious soft alternative.

Cooking the couscous in the top pot at the same time will mean your meal is ready when you are ready to eat.

1 tbsp olive oil , plus extra for drizzling

2 medium onions, peeled and sliced

2 cloves garlic, peeled and finely diced

400 g tin tomatoes, diced

500 ml red wine

500 ml chicken stock

3 tbsp red wine vinegar

3 bay leaves

1 tsp thyme, dried

150 g black olives, pitted and drained

1 kg squid tubes, sliced

500 ml water (440ml for ordinary couscous)

1 tbsp butter

½ tsp salt

250 g giant couscous (if ordinary couscous use same dry weight)

Salt and black pepper to taste

1. Heat the oil in the inner pot over a medium-low heat, add the onions and cook until the onions are soft.
2. Add the tomatoes, red wine, chicken stock, red wine vinegar, bay leaves and dried thyme. Bring to the boil and add the olives and squid. Bring back to the boil.
3. Give the casserole a stir, turn off the heat, place the inner pot into the outer Thermal Container. Shut the lid and leave to thermally cook without power for a minimum of 1 hour.

Cooking the couscous in the top pot

1. Bring the water and butter to the boil in the top pot, and stir in the couscous and salt.
2. Turn off the heat, open the vacuum-insulated Thermal Container and remove the lid from the inner pot, then place the top pot into the inner pot.
3. Put on the top pot lid and close the outer container.
4. Leave to thermal cook without power for the same length of time as the squid.

To serve   1. Fluff the couscous with a fork.

2. Check the seasoning of the squid and adjust if necessary.

3. Serve with a nice Greek salad

serves: 4   *minimum thermal cooking time without power: 1 hour*

69

Coronation Chicken
Recipe 49 - 4th June 2013

In 1953 Constance Spry and Rosemary Hume, both principals of the Cordon Bleu Cookery School in London, created a dish to celebrate the coronation of Queen Elizabeth II. Preparing the food for the coronation banquet, Constance Spry proposed the recipe that would later become known as coronation chicken.

I have in this recipe taken the original and made a number of changes to suit the thermal cooker but without losing that lovely creamy curry taste. Coronation chicken is lovely with a salad or in sandwiches.

500 g chicken, cut into strips

1 medium onion, chopped

1 tbsp curry powder

100 ml white wine

1 bay leaf

½ lemon (juice only)

3 tbsp mango chutney

250 ml mayonnaise

50 ml double cream

1   Prepare to use the top pot as a Bain Marie by filling the inner pot with water up to approximately half an inch above the trivet, then bring the water to the boil with the inner pot lid on.

2. Once boiling, put it in the outer insulated Thermal Container and shut the lid.

3. Add all the ingredients except for the mayonnaise and cream to the top pot and mix well.

4. Remove the inner pot from the outer insulated Thermal Container, put the top pot in the inner pot (it hangs inside the rim) and heat the inner pot until it comes back to the boil.

5. Lower the heat and simmer for 5 minutes, stirring the contents of the top pot from time to time.

6. Turn off the heat, place the inner pot back into the vacuum-insulated outer Thermal Container, shut the lid and leave to thermally cook without power for a minimum of 2 to 3 hours.

7. Once cooked, remove the top pot and leave to cool before putting in the fridge to really chill.

8. When ready to serve, stir in the mayonnaise and cream.

serves: 4   minimum thermal cooking time without power: 2 hours

Pork Adobo with Quail Eggs

Recipe 50 - 13th June 2013

This recipe came about because Sarah asked on Mr D's Friends of Thermal Cooking for a recipe to use some of her quail eggs.

Adobo is a very famous Filipino dish and has become the national dish of the Philippines. There are many versions and if you enjoy this one, there is a chicken version in my cookbook, 'Mr D's Thermal Cookbook'.

1 kg Pork cubes

1 medium onion, chopped

200 ml soy sauce

200 ml white vinegar

6 cloves garlic, crushed

3 bay leaves

1 tsp paprika

400 ml coconut cream

1 ½ cups rice

24 quail eggs, hard boiled and peeled

1. Add all the ingredients except the quail eggs to the inner pot and bring to the boil.
2. Skim off any impurities that form on the surface and turn down to a simmer.
3. Simmer for 5 minutes with the lid on.
4. Turn off the heat and place the inner pot into the vacuum-insulated outer Thermal Container.
5. Shut the lid and leave to thermally cook without power for a minimum of 3 hours.

Cooking the rice in the top pot

7. Add the rice and three cups of water to the top pot and bring to the boil, stir and turn down the heat and simmer for 1 minute.
8. Turn off the heat, open the vacuum-insulated Thermal Container and remove the lid from the inner container. Place the top pot into the inner pot.
9. Leave to thermal cook without power for the same length of time as the pork adobo.

To serve

1. Before serving, stir in the quail eggs (being careful not to break them up).
2. Serve the pork adobo on a bed of rice and some stir fry or steamed pak choi and broccoli spears.

serves: 4   minimum thermal cooking time without power: 3 hours

Sophie's Lamb Tagine
Recipe 51 - 18th June 2013

The recipe this week is provided by Sophie, who will be cooking for the crew of Jubilant during this year's Fastnet race.

Sophie kindly brought some tagine for us to try at the Midsummer Motorhome Show in Exeter, and it was so popular that I decided it had to be included in my weekly recipes.

Because of the sugars in this dish, it goes into the pot super hot and stays hot in Mr D's Thermal Cooker hours longer than most meals.

2 tbsp rapeseed oil	2 x 400 g tins chopped tomatoes
2 large onions, chopped into small pieces	500 ml tomato juice or pasata
1 tsp coriander	2 cloves garlic, finely chopped
1 tsp cayenne pepper	120 g dried apricots, cut in half
1 tsp black pepper	60 g dates, cut in half
1 tsp paprika	60 g sultanas or raisins
1 tsp ground ginger	100 g flaked almonds
1 tsp turmeric	1 pinch saffron stamens
1 tsp cinnamon	500 ml lamb stock
1.5 kg lamb, cut into chunks. Shoulder is good, but Sophie uses scrag end or neck, as it cooks for so long and is far tastier.	3 tbsp clear honey
	½ cup parsley, chopped

1 Heat the oil in the inner pot over a medium heat.
2 Add the onions and fry until soft.
3 Add the coriander, parsley, cayenne pepper, black pepper, paprika, ground ginger, turmeric and cinnamon. Stir for a couple of minutes.
4 Add the lamb and mix with the spices and onions.
5 Add the tins of tomatoes, tomato juice or pasata to the meat and cook until it starts to bubble a bit.
6 Add the garlic, fruit and rest of the ingredients.
7 Bring to the boil while stirring. Once boiling, turn down and simmer for 5 minutes with the lid on.
8 Turn off the heat and place the Inner Pot into the vacuum-insulated Outer Pot.
9 Shut the lid and leave to thermally cook without power for a minimum of 3 hours.

Cooking couscous in the top pot if you have one.

1. Add couscous and water according to the packet.
2. Open the vacuum-insulated Outer Pot and remove the lid from the Inner Pot. Place the Top Pot into the Inner Pot, put the lid on the Top Pot and close the Outer Pot.
3. Leave to thermal cook without power for the same length of time as the tagine.

serves: 4 - 5   minimum thermal cooking time without power: 3 hours

Indian Roast Beef & Vegetable Curry

Recipe 52 - 26th June 2013

This recipe is adapted from one by Atul Kochher, one of only two Indian Chefs in the world to be awarded a coveted Michelin Star.

I decided to serve Atul Kochhars Indian Roast Beef with a South Indian vegetable curry, which I made in the top pot. If, however, you do not have a top pot, then you can increase the size of beef and increase the beef stock a little.

The beef is thermally cooked for a long time, so it melts in the mouth.

Serves 4   minimum thermal cooking time without power: 5 hours

750 g beef joint (if not using a Top Pot increase the beef size to 1.2kg *)

Marinade for the beef

25 g garlic, crushed

25 g root ginger, grated

10 black peppercorns, coarsely ground

1 tsp turmeric

1 tsp round cumin

1 tsp ground coriander

1 tsp salt

2 tbsp rapeseed oil

Ingredients for cooking the beef

25 g garlic, crushed

25 g root ginger, grated

1 tbsp wine vinegar

1 tsp chilli flakes

6 cloves

2 bay leaves

5 cm cinnamon stick

1 ¼ litres beef stock (if not using the top pot, increase this to enough to cover the beef)

½ tsp salt

* If using a Top Pot to cook the vegetable curry or rice, check that the beef is no bigger that 6.5cms thick so it will fit under the Top Pot. If it is larger, cut it into two.

To marinade

Prick the beef all over so it can absorb the marinade, mix all the marinade ingredients together, rub over the beef and leave to marinade in the fridge for a minimum of 2 hours. Overnight would be better

Cooking the beef

1. Put the ingredients and stock into the Inner Pot, then place in the beef and bring it to the boil. Once boiling, turn the heat down to simmer for 5 minutes with the lid on.
2. Turn off the heat, place the Inner Pot into the vacuum-insulated Outer Pot, shut the lid and leave to thermally cook without power for a minimum of 5 hours.

Ingredients for South Indian Vegetable Curry

1 medium onion, chopped

2 tsp black mustard seeds

8-10 curry leaves

1 green chilli, thinly sliced

2 tsp root ginger, grated

1 tsp ground turmeric

2 tsp ground cumin

6 black peppercorns

2 carrots cut into batons

1 courgette cut into batons

100 g green beans, trimmed and cut in 3 cm lengths

1 large potato, cut into small cubes

150 ml coconut cream

250 ml vegetable stock

salt & pepper

Cooking the vegetable curry in the top pot

1. Put all the ingredients for the South Indian vegetable curry into the Top Pot, stir, and bring to the boil on the hob.
2. Once boiling, turn down to simmer for 5 minutes, then turn off the heat, open the vacuum-insulated Outer Pot and remove the lid from the Inner Pot. Place the Top Pot into the Inner Pot and put the Top Pot lid on.
3. Shut the Outer Pot and leave to thermal cook without power for the same length of time as the beef.

To serve

1. Slice the beef and serve with rice and the vegetable curry.
2. Pour some of the liquid the beef was cooked in over the beef before serving.
3. Serve with naan bread. You can also add a vegetable curry on the side.

Cooking the rice in the top pot.

1. Add 2 cups rice and 3 cups water to the Top Pot, bring to the boil, stir, then turn down the heat and simmer for 1 minute.
2. Turn off the heat, open the Outer Pot, place the Top Pot into the Inner Pot, put the lid on the Top Pot, shut the lid of the Outer Pot, then leave to thermal cook without power for an hour, or, if on top of another meal, leave for the same time as the main meal.

Recipes
Alphabetical index

To find more recipes for thermal cooking
and more information about thermal cooking and Mr D's cookware
go to: www.MrDsCookware.co.uk
or email: mail@mrdscookware.co.uk